The Ultimate
Gaelic Football

Gavin Mortimer

This book was conceived, edited and designed for Gill & Macmillan by
Tony Potter Publishing Ltd
tonypotter.com

Illustrators: John Cooper & Brett Hudson
Editorial consultants: Noel Quinlan & Les Fitzmaurice

All photos © www.inpho.ie

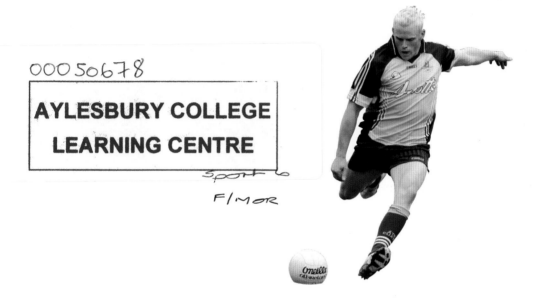

GILL & MACMILLAN LTD
Hume Avenue, Park West, Dublin 12
with associated companies throughout the world
www.gillmacmillan.ie

First published 2008

Contents

Kicking off

Colm Cooper scores for Kerry in the 2007 All-Ireland Final

Romance, drama, passion, excitement, controversy... Gaelic Football has it all! Ireland's awesome game just gets more thrilling each year.

A day out for Dubs fans at the 2006 Leinster Final

The Ultimate Guide to Gaelic Football reflects some of this special atmosphere. Whether you're an up-and-coming hotshot with your sights set on scoring the winning goal in the All-Ireland Final in front of 80,000 delirious fans at Croke Park, or just someone who enjoys watching the likes of Kieran Donaghy and Alan Brogan on the television, this book will have something for you.

You'll find out all about some of the greatest ever All-Ireland finals, learn the skills of the game, from soloing to shooting, discover football's fascinating history and pass judgement on our 'Dream Team' – today's top talent!

It's doesn't matter which team you support: as long as you're a football fan, then read on!

Gaelic's Gone Global

Canada: Gaelic Football has a loyal following in Canada among men and women, and at an international women's tournament in 2005, Canada beat Britain in the final.

Scotland: Football is making a resurgence in Scotland with teams all over the country. In addition there are now women's teams, and youth football is growing in popularity.

USA: Irish immigrants brought football across the Atlantic and matches were being played in San Francisco as early as the 1850s. There is an annual North American football championship and in recent years, Chicago's Wolfe Tones have been the dominant team.

Ireland: A version of Gaelic Football was played in Ireland in the 14th century and records show the game being played by 1670. The first county games were reported to have taken place in the early 1800s before the GAA was formed in 1884.

New York: Gaelic Football has always been particularly strong in New York and there are over 30 sides in the NY GAA league, with Gaelic Park the atmospheric centrepiece stadium.

England: Outside Ireland nowhere has football a prouder tradition than London. In the early 1900s London played five All-Ireland finals, with most players hailing from Cork. One of the most famous was Sam Maguire. London entered the National Football League in 1993 and the game continues to thrive in the British capital.

Europe: The European GAA is expanding at an astonishing rate, with four annual pan-European championships and shield rounds including teams from Sweden, Germany, Hungary and France.

Asia: There are football teams all over Asia in countries such as Japan and South Korea. But at the 2007 Asian Gaelic Games it was Hong Kong who lifted the trophy, beating Singapore in the final.

New Zealand: Football has been played in Auckland since the 1940s. After the formation of the GAA of Australia in 1974, Auckland and Hutt Valley joined, and so the GAA of Australasia was created.

Australia: There were reports of football games being played on the goldfields of Victoria in the 1850s but it took another 100 years until associations were formed. In 1971 the first interstate championships were played in Melbourne. State championships continue to flourish today, with Western Australia riding high in men's and women's championships.

The Football Field

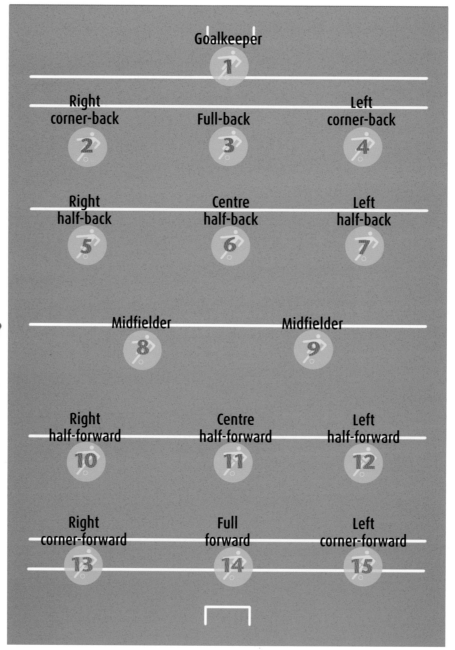

Goalkeeper
1

Right corner-back **2** | Full-back **3** | Left corner-back **4**

Right half-back **5** | Centre half-back **6** | Left half-back **7**

Midfielder **8** | Midfielder **9**

Right half-forward **10** | Centre half-forward **11** | Left half-forward **12**

Right corner-forward **13** | Full forward **14** | Left corner-forward **15**

did you know?

A Gaelic Football pitch is 137m long and 82m wide, which makes it bigger than either a soccer pitch or an American Football field!

There are 15 players on a Gaelic Football team: a goalkeeper, who wears a different colour jersey, six backs, two midfielders and six forwards. What's your position?

A Gaelic Football match lasts for 60 minutes (two halves of 30 minutes), except for senior inter-county games which go on for 70 minutes.

Ross Munnelly grabs a goal for Laois against Dublin

The goalposts are shaped like the letter H with a net attached to the bottom half. In front of each goal are two rectangles marked on the pitch. The goalkeeper may not be challenged in the smaller of the two rectangles, although he is allowed to be challenged for possession of the ball.

A penalty kick is awarded to the attacking side if a defender commits an aggressive foul in the larger of the two rectangles, or if he commits any type of foul in the small rectangle. (See pages 12 and 14 for more on fouls!)

There are white lines marked across the pitch at 13m, 20m and 45m intervals in both halves, and a penalty kick is taken from the 13m line.

One point is scored when the ball goes between the posts and over the crossbar. If the ball goes under the crossbar and into the net, a goal is scored which is worth three points.

The ball is similar to a soccer ball but slightly heavier and there are several rules about how the ball is passed. The ball must not be thrown but must be struck with either the fist or the palm.

Players are not allowed to pick the ball directly off the ground and the ball is not allowed to be bounced twice in a row. Players are not permitted to take more than four steps without either releasing, bouncing or toe-tapping it.

Opponents can tackle the ball carrier by either trying to slap the ball from their grasp or by the 'shoulder to shoulder' tackle – see page 37 for tackle tips!

did you know?

A Gaelic football must weigh not more than 485g and not less than 450g.

The Dream Team

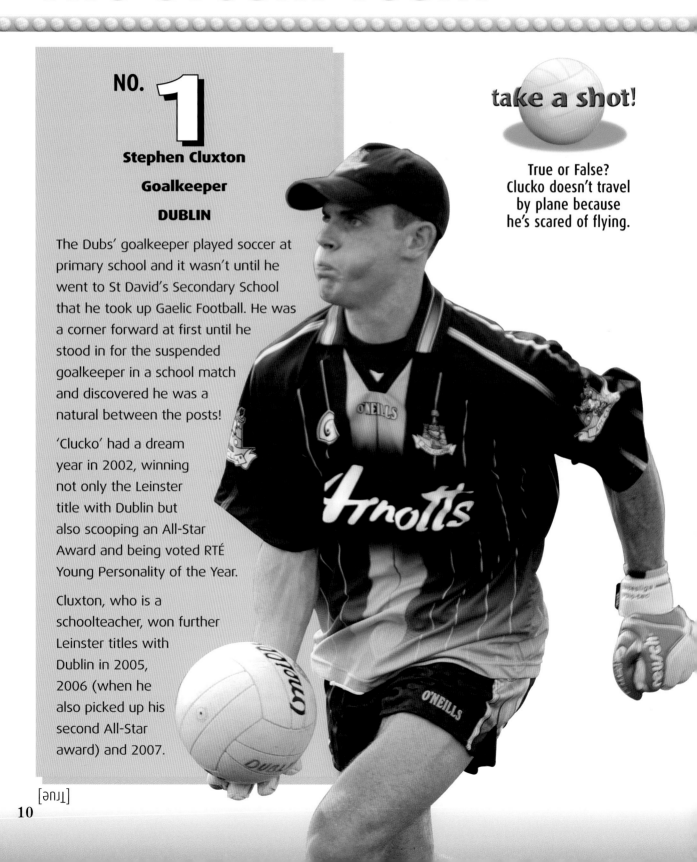

NO. 1

Stephen Cluxton

Goalkeeper

DUBLIN

The Dubs' goalkeeper played soccer at primary school and it wasn't until he went to St David's Secondary School that he took up Gaelic Football. He was a corner forward at first until he stood in for the suspended goalkeeper in a school match and discovered he was a natural between the posts!

'Clucko' had a dream year in 2002, winning not only the Leinster title with Dublin but also scooping an All-Star Award and being voted RTÉ Young Personality of the Year.

Cluxton, who is a schoolteacher, won further Leinster titles with Dublin in 2005, 2006 (when he also picked up his second All-Star award) and 2007.

take a shot!

True or False?
Clucko doesn't travel
by plane because
he's scared of flying.

[ənɹʇ]

Goalkeeping Gods

There's more to being a cool 'keeper than preventing points being scored.

Look at the great goalkeepers in football history, from the likes of Dan O'Keefe in the 1930s, to today's stars such as Diarmuid Murphy and Stephen Cluxton, and what have they all got in common?

That's right, all-round talent. Of course, the most important skill for a 'keeper is just that: keep the ball out of the goal! Remember how David Clarke won the All-Ireland semifinal for Mayo against Dublin in 2006 by saving Mark Vaughan's free in the last few minutes? Incredible!

Stopping shots requires great reflexes and a good eye – you need to be able to judge the flight of the ball, and then move quickly to keep it out of the goal.

It will help your goalkeeping if you study your opponents. Learn which forwards are dangerous close in, which players are left-footed or right-footed. Try to anticipate how they will go for goal.

Another skill all goalkeepers can improve with practice is the kick-out. This is how, with one big, booming kick, you can turn defence into attack. Instead of you defending your goal, it becomes the opposition 'keeper under pressure!

You have to be courageous to be a first-class 'keeper. You don't see the likes of 'Clucko' shirking a high ball because he's scared he might be sent flying by a fiery forward. Once a goalkeeper goes up for a high ball there's no going back…if anyone is going to come down with a bump, make sure it's the forward. So remember, be brave, be decisive, and you're on your way to being a goalkeeping God!

Diarmuid Murphy of Kerry is one of football's great shot stoppers

Gaelic Gobbledegook

Like all sports, Gaelic Football has its own funny phrases. So do you know your toe-tap from your throw-in?

1 Charge: A player can make a shoulder to shoulder charge against an opponent as long as he has one foot on the ground, and his opponent is playing the ball. A charge is also allowed if both players are pursuing the ball to play it.

2 Lift: A player must use his foot or feet to transfer the ball from the ground to his hands. He is not allowed to use his hands direct.

3 Solo: The action of releasing the ball from the hand to the foot and kicking it (tapping it) back into the hands.

4 Overcarry: When a player takes more than the permitted four steps while holding the ball in his hands. This is a technical foul, punishable by a free kick.

5 Overhold: When a player keeps the ball longer than is necessary to take four steps.

6 Throw: When a player passes the ball from his hands without clearly striking it.

7 Throw in: To throw the ball up over the heads of one player from each team. The throw in is also used to start the game at the beginning of each half.

8 Divot: A small mound of turf on the pitch on which the ball is placed prior to a kick being taken.

9 A '45': A method of restarting play after a defender has put the ball wide of the goals. A forward may take a '45' on the 45m line, level with where the ball went wide.

The Dream Team

NO. 2
Ryan McMenamin
Right corner-back
TYRONE

McMenamin is an attacking corner-back and never afraid to run at the opposition. A tough competitor who relishes marking football's top forwards, he was a member of the first ever Tyrone side to win an All-Ireland title in 2003, and he was also present in 2005 when they repeated their success.

As well as the All-Ireland medals, McMenamin has won three Ulster titles with the Red Hand County (including 2007), and in 2005 he collected his first All-Star award.

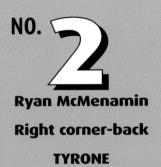

take a shot!

True or False?
Ryan McMenamin was born in the USA.

NO. 4
Karl Lacey
Left corner-back
DONEGAL

The 23-year-old Lacey is one of the up-and-coming talents in Gaelic Football, having won a county championship medal for Four Masters in 2003. He then broke into the Donegal side and helped them reach the quarter-final of the 2006 All-Ireland. Lacey was at the heart of the Donegal defence when they won the 2007 National Football League for the first time.

[False: He was born in Canada]

Karl Lacey

The Pass Masters

Football is a game of teamwork and nothing emphasises this more than the pass – combining with your team-mates to get the ball in the back of the opposition net.

There are two types of pass using the hand. One is called the fist pass and the other is the hand pass, which actually uses the palm.

In fact, the hand pass has been a source of controversy over the years in Gaelic Football. In 1945 the open hand pass was banned, but then it was reinstated the next year. However, in 1950 the pass was once again ruled illegal, only for it to be reintroduced in 1975. Then, in 1981, the GAA decided to keep the open hand pass but forbid its use to score goals.

Why do players sometimes pass using the foot and at other times the hand? Well, you can get more power and distance using the boot, but what you can't always get is accuracy. Passing with the hand might not make you as many metres upfield, but more often than not the ball isn't going to fall into the clutches of the opposition because you can control it more.

Remember that the referee must see a distinct striking motion when you make a pass. If he doesn't and he judges that you threw the ball, then he'll award a free kick against you for a technical foul. For goodness sake, it isn't rugby!

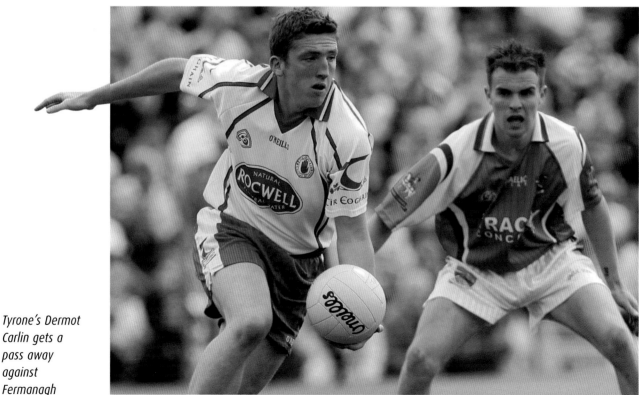

Tyrone's Dermot Carlin gets a pass away against Fermanagh

1 Clench your fist and rest your thumb against the outside of your index finger. You now have a compact area to strike the ball, formed by the middle bones of your fingers and the base of your hand.

2 If you're right-handed, hold the ball in the palm of your left hand (and vice versa for left-handed players) which should be out in front of your body so that the hand that strikes the ball can generate sufficient power.

3 Keeping your eyes on the ball, lean forward slightly and bring your striking hand through in a swinging motion while ensuring the hand that holds the ball is steady. Once your fist makes contact with the ball, follow through with your striking hand for maximum power.

Cork's Graham Canty in action

Go Solo

Nothing gets the blood pumping and the heart racing as much as a super solo run!

Galway's Michael Donnellan goes on another super solo

When the public voted in 2005 for their top 20 favourite GAA moments of all time, do you know what was No.1? That's right, Michael Donnellan's stunning solo run for Galway against Kildare in the 1998 All-Ireland Final that led to his team scoring a priceless point.

The thing is, Donnellan made soloing look easy! In fact, it's harder than it looks, but with these top tips you might find yourself 'Doing a Donnellan' in a few years' time!

Before we go any further, don't forget it's important to remember that in football the player in possession of the ball can only carry it for a maximum of four steps. Any more and you have committed an 'overcarry' foul. Before you

can say 'Sorry!' you'll hear the referee's whistle and there'll be a free kick against your team.

So if you have the ball and you fancy going on a solo run, don't forget that if you want to go more than four steps, you have to either bounce the ball on the ground back to yourself, or drop the ball on to your foot and kick it back to yourself, which is called a solo.

HOWEVER, a player is not allowed to bounce the ball on the ground twice in succession. He must alternate bouncing the ball on the ground with soloing it, but you'll be pleased to know that you can solo the ball from hand to foot and back again as many times as you wish.

The hardest thing about soloing is to run fast while moving the ball from hand to foot and back to hand. It requires a lot of concentration, not to mention coordination. If at first you find you drop the ball a lot, don't worry and certainly don't give up! As you practise more, your coordination will improve and so will your speed.

Remember to keep your eyes on the ball the whole time

Top Training Tips

Why not start out by practising soloing while standing still. Drop the ball on to your foot and get used to kicking it back into your hands. When you've mastered the kick and catch, then start to walk and solo. As you feel more confident, increase your speed until you're 'Doing a Donnellan'!

1 Hold the ball in two hands and keep your eyes on the ball as you continue running.

2 Keep an upright posture and drop the ball (don't hurl or throw it!) on to the kicking foot while watching the ball.

3 As the foot comes into contact with the ball, curl your toes towards you so that you end up flicking the ball back into your hands. Remember to keep your eyes on the ball at all times!

4 When the ball is back in your hands then you can look up and see whether you continue soloing or whether you pass to a team-mate in a shooting position.

Demon Defenders

Courage and determination, and a dislike of goalscorers – that's what you need to be a demon defender!

Even though there are six defensive positions in football, they all share the same objective on the football field – to stop the opposition scoring points by marking the forwards out of the game.

Perhaps being a defender isn't as glamorous as being a forward – it's the goals and points that make the record books after all – but they are just as important! Look at Kerry's Seamus Moynihan, for example, or Graham Canty; two defenders who have never been afraid to put their bodies on the line to stop the opposition scoring. They're respected by friend and foe alike.

In last season's All-Ireland semi against Cork, Kerry's Moynihan stopped a certain goal with a great bit of defence that was just as crucial to his side as the points scored by Colm Cooper.

Blocking and tackling are obviously two of the biggest skills needed to be a feared defender, both of which require bravery and determination. But you also need to be able to time your challenge, so that you take the ball away from your opponent without giving away a foul!

Don't just think being a defender is all about stopping the opposition attacking! The very best defenders like getting on the score sheet themselves – look at Ger Spillane – or they enjoy launching counter-attacks by sending the ball quickly out of defence. Tyrone's Ryan McMenamin is a great example of a defender who sticks like glue to his opposing forward, but at the first opportunity he gets, he breaks out and looks to set up a goalscoring chance for one of his forwards.

Seamus Moynihan gets to grips with Cork's Sean O'Brien

The Dream Team

take a shot!

True or False?
Canty was out with
a shoulder injury.

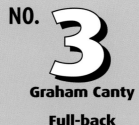

NO. 3

Graham Canty

Full-back

CORK

Cork fans breathed a sigh of relief early in 2007 when Graham Canty returned to action after ten months sidelined with injury. The hard-as-nails full-back injured himself in helping Cork to victory over Kerry in the Munster Final replay, having been the defensive rock throughout the early part of the season. However, when the two sides met again in the 2007 All-Ireland Final, not even Canty could prevent a Kingdom victory.

Canty first came to prominence in 1999 in his first season with Cork Under-21s, and two years later he captained them to glory in the Munster Final. That same season, 2001, Canty established himself in the senior team and he looks set to be a regular for years to come.

[False: It was a knee injury]

*Shane Lennon of Louth with
Graham Canty of Cork*

Football Facts

Impress your friends with our fantastic football facts.

In 1990 Teddy McCarthy of Cork became the first player to win All-Ireland hurling and football medals in the same year.

The worst case of wayward shooting came in the 1960 Munster Football Final when Kerry (3-15) beat Waterford (0-8) and were guilty of 27 wides.

The first floodlit GAA match was staged by Burren at their Mourne playing field in 1975.

Noel Meehan helped Caltra to success in the 2004 club final

When Kildare beat Kerry to win the 1905 All-Ireland Final the result was telephoned back to Kildare – the first case of the telephone being used to report a GAA score.

When Caltra (0-13) beat An Gaeltacht (0-12) in the 2004 club final, 11 of Caltra's points were scored by the Meehan brothers with Michael getting six and captain Noel, five.

In 1994 Stephen Calnan scored the quickest goal in club final history when he netted after ten seconds for Nemo Rangers against Castlebar Mitchels.

Ray Cunningham's point for Cavan against Derry in the 1997 final was awarded by the referee even though TV replays showed it was clearly wide. Cavan won the match by a point for their first Ulster title in 28 years.

Teddy McCarthy was a double champion in 1990 for Cork

The first penalty in an All-Ireland Final was in 1948 when Padraig Carney scored for Mayo against Cavan, but Cavan still won by a point.

Arguably the most successful All-Ireland star was Pierce Grace. He won three hurling medals with Kilkenny from 1911 to 1913, having won two football medals with Dublin in 1906 and 1907.

The Kingdom of Kerry

They're the greatest side in Gaelic Football history, the men from Kerry in green and gold who have won an amazing 35 All-Ireland titles.

Kerry's Mikey Sheehy receives support from Ger Power in the 1986 All-Ireland win against Tyrone

Kerry is one of the larger counties in terms of size and population, and down the years the Kingdom, as it's better known, has produced many of the greats of the game.

One of the first Kerry legends was Dick Fitzgerald, in whose honour the stadium in Killarney is named. He was a member of the Kerry side who won their first All-Ireland title in 1903.

The 1930s was a memorable decade for Kerry as they won five All-Ireland medals, thanks to, for example, goalkeeper Dan O'Keefe, full-back Joe Keohane and forward J J Landers. More success followed in the 1940s and then 1950s with Sean Murphy inspirational in defence as Kerry won three more medals.

But it was in the late 1970s that Kerry began to dominate Gaelic Football as no other side had ever done. In Pat Spillane and Mikey Sheehy, the Kingdom had two players who would later be named in the GAA Team of the Millennium. All-Ireland titles came in 1978, 1979, 1980, 1981, 1984, 1985 and 1986 – a remarkable record.

More recently Kerry have been crowned All-Ireland champs in 2000, 2004, 2006 and 2007, leaving the rest of the GAA in no doubt that the Kingdom is as strong as ever!

Kerry have won an incredible 72 Munster Championships, including the 2007 title.

Timeline

1884 On November 1 the GAA is formed in Thurles by Michael Cusack and six other Irishmen.

1887 Limerick 1-4 beat Louth 0-3 in the first All-Ireland Football Final.

1888 The number of players on a team is reduced from 21 a side to 17 a side.

1892 Until 1892 a goal was worth more than any number of points, but in this year it is equated to five points. Three years later, in 1895, a goal is reduced to three points.

1895 Linesmen use flags for the first time to draw the referee's attention.

1895 Tipperary defeat Meath by a point in the first All-Ireland Final to be played on what is now Croke Park (it was known as Jones's Road at the time).

1903 The scoring area is reduced from 54 to 45 feet (16.5m to 13.7m).

1910 Point posts are abolished and the goalposts are set at 21 feet (6.5m) apart.

1913 The number of players on a team is reduced from 17 to 15 a side.

1923 Numbered jerseys are introduced.

1925 Players no longer have to play for the county in which they live but can 'declare' for their native county.

1935 The size of the pitch is reduced from 170 to 160 yards (155.5m to 146m).

1940 The penalty kick is introduced.

1947 The All-Ireland Final is held at the Polo Grounds, New York: the first time it has been staged outside Ireland.

1950 The open hand pass is outlawed.

1962 The All-Ireland semifinal between Dublin and Kerry is the first match to be broadcast by RTÉ.

1970 All-Ireland semifinals and finals are increased from 60 to 70 minutes.

1975 The open hand pass is reintroduced.

2000 Blood substitutes are allowed and substitutes are increased from 3 to 5.

The Dream Team

NO. 6

Ger Spillane

Centre-back

CORK

What a season Ger Spillane enjoyed in 2006! That was the year he finally established himself in the Cork side, having played several seasons for the junior team.

First Spillane was voted Man of the Match in the Munster Football Final against Kerry, and then he picked up a similar award for his performance in the All-Ireland quarterfinal against Donegal.

It was Spillane's injury-time point that snatched a dramatic winner for the Rebels and although they later went out in the semis, Spillane's form resulted in his first ever All-Star award. Even though he didn't enjoy the best of days when the Rebels lost to Kerry in the 2007 All-Ireland Final, Spillane is sure to win more All-Stars.

Ger Spillane

take a shot!

True or False?
Spillane won a
Cork Junior Hurling
Championship medal
in 2004.

[True: For Ballygarvan]

Playing for Kicks

One of the things that makes Gaelic Football such a great sport is its combination of kicking and handling. Rugby relies on good hands, soccer on sound feet, but in Gaelic Football you need to have both!

There are three main types of kick used in Gaelic Football – the free kick, the punt and the long kicked pass. We're going to show you how you can improve all three!

Free kicks are awarded for fouls and often they present the side with a great chance to score some points. Just look at Dublin's Mark Vaughan and the five frees he scored against Laois in the final of the Leinster Championship. Frees are also a good way of getting the ball in the danger area for one of your forwards to fire a home goal.

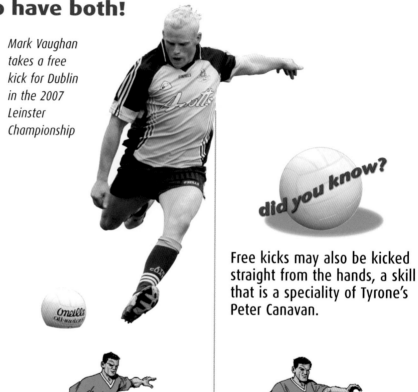

Mark Vaughan takes a free kick for Dublin in the 2007 Leinster Championship

did you know?

Free kicks may also be kicked straight from the hands, a skill that is a speciality of Tyrone's Peter Canavan.

Placing the ball

Place the ball on the spot indicated by the referee and then take a few steps back to give yourself a good run at the ball. Glance up at the posts one last time and then focus on the ball.

Running up to the ball

Run up to the ball, keeping your eyes on it the whole time, and plant your non-kicking foot alongside the ball with your arms slightly outstretched for balance.

Kicking the ball

The toe of your foot should make contact near the bottom of the ball in an attempt to lift the ball up and over the bar. Don't forget, keep your eyes on the ball and not the posts!

24

The punt and the long kicked pass differ from a free kick because they are kicked out of hand and not from the ground. They are ideal for passing to a team-mate as well as scoring points.

Meath's Cian Ward kicks a point in the 2007 Leinster Championship

The long kicked pass

Hold the ball in two hands and point your shoulder where you want to kick the ball so you are side-on to the target. If you are right-footed you should point with your left shoulder (and vice-versa). As you go to kick the ball, transfer it to your right hand and extend your left for balance. Drop the ball on to your right foot and strike it with the inside of your foot so that you 'hook' the ball across your body. Follow through with your kicking leg so that your foot points to where the ball is going.

The punt

Many of the same techniques apply to the punt as to the hook, except when you punt the ball downfield you are not side-on but front-on to your target. The first thing to do is choose where you want to kick the ball. So look up and pick a target. Then, keeping your eyes on the ball which is held in both hands, take a step forward and drop it on to your foot. The part of the foot that kicks the ball is the instep – that's the area between the bottom of your laces and the toe of your boot. Follow through with your leg for maximum power.

The Dream Team

NO. 5

Tomás Ó Sé
Right half-back
KERRY

Tomás Ó Sé won All-Ireland medals with Kerry in 2000, 2004, 2006 and 2007, having sat on the bench as a teenager in the Kingdom's 1997 triumph.

Hailing from a famous football family, Ó Sé's elder brother, Darragh, has won two All-Star awards while younger brother Marc is also a player of great promise.

Tomás's two All-Star awards came in 2004 and 2005, and don't bet against more heading his way before long!

Kerry's Tomás Ó Sé

take a shot!

True or False? Ó Sé's uncle, Paidi, was an All-Ireland winner with Kerry as both a player and manager.

NO. 7

Paul Galvin
Left half-back
KERRY

A fiery half-back, Galvin was at the heart of the Kerry defence when they beat Mayo to win the All-Ireland Final in 2004.

That same year Galvin also helped Ireland defeat Australia in the International Rules and then topped a memorable season with his first All-Star award.

Galvin was sent off in the 2006 All-Ireland quarterfinal against Armagh, but was there for Kerry's Final triumph that year. In 2007 he sent over a superb score in the Final victory over Cork.

Paul Galvin

[True]

The Dublin Dynamos

Dublin are one of the great football sides, and even though they haven't won an All-Ireland Final since 1995, they picked up their third Leinster Championship title in a row in 2007.

It was way back in 1891 that the Dubs first won an All-Ireland title when they beat Cork in front of 2000 fans at Clonturk Park. Before the end of the 19th century they had won five more championships, including three in a row from 1897 to 1899.

The Boys in Blue claimed another hat-trick of All-Ireland wins in 1921, '22 and '23 with stars such as Frank Burke and captain Paddy Carey at the heart of their success.

The 1930s and 1940s weren't kind to Dublin but they tasted more All-Ireland glory in 1958, thanks in no small part to forward Kevin Heffernan, one of Dublin's greatest ever players.

Heffernan then turned to management and proved just as successful off the pitch as he had been on it! Under his guidance, Dublin wrote the most glorious chapter in their long and proud history.

With, for example, Kevin Moran, Bernie Brogan and Jimmy Keaveney terrorising opponents, the Dubs won four All-Ireland titles between 1974 and 1983 and also scooped four Leinster titles on the trot.

Dublin's last All-Ireland title

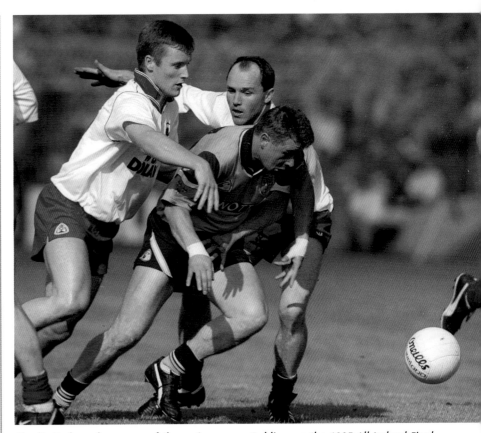

Charlie Redmond was one of the main reasons Dublin won the 1995 All-Ireland Final

came in 1995 from a team built around the skills of 'keeper John O'Leary and the firepower up front of Charlie Redmond.

Since then Dublin fans have played a waiting game, but with Stephen Cluxton, Alan Brogan and Mark Vaughan in the current side, they might not have to wait too much longer!

did you know?

Only Kerry with 34 have won more All-Ireland titles than Dublin's 22 triumphs.

All-Ireland Action

The very first All-Ireland Football Final was held in 1887, when Limerick beat Louth at Clonskeagh. Now we're in the third century of football finals but one thing hasn't changed – the nerve-tingling, nail-biting excitement of Final day at Croke Park. Here are ten of the top finals ever played.

To the victor the spoils! The Sam Maguire Cup

1895 Tipperary 0-4 Meath 0-3, Jones's Road (8000)

This was Willie Ryan's match with the Arravale Rovers' star scoring all of Tipperary's points, including a spectacular effort when he chased and caught his own kick and launched it over the posts for the equalising score. Ryan scored the winner from a free with seven minutes left on the clock.

1903 Kerry 0-8 Kildare 0-2 (second replay), Croke Park (20,000)

It took three matches for Kerry to defeat Kildare in a series of games that were all classics in their own right. The cry 'Up Kerry!' originated this year and Kildare dyed their boots white to match the colour of their new shirts. Kildare 'keeper Jack Fitzgerald was the hero in the first replay with a brilliant late save to deny Jim O'Gorman, but in the second replay Kerry's Dick Fitzgerald inspired his boys to victory in a dramatic match.

1926 Kerry 1-3 Kildare 0-6, Croke Park (37,500)

A record 37,500 fans filled Croke Park to witness a fantastic final between Kerry and Kildare. Paul Doyle had opened Kildare's account with an early point and after 28 minutes of a tense second half they seemed set to lift the Sam Maguire Cup. But then up popped Kerry's Bill Gorman to score at the death and force the match into a reply. Tragically, the Kerry centre half-back Jack Murphy, who was superb in the final, fell ill with pneumonia and died before the rematch. His Kingdom team-mates won the replay in his honour.

1955 Kerry 0-12 Dublin 1-6, Croke Park (87,102)

The hero for Kerry was corner-back Jerome O'Shea. He pulled off two magnificent saves in the second half, minutes from time, but it wasn't enough to overturn a Kerry lead that was built on the points of the cool-headed Tadhgie Lyne.

1960 Down 2-10 Kerry 0-8, Croke Park (87,768)

Down had never made it to the final before and they were against All-Ireland old hands, Kerry. The atmosphere turned white-hot early in the second half when Dan McCartan tried to lob the Kerry 'keeper from 40 yards. The goalkeeper seemed to have the ball but then dropped it over the line. Two minutes later Down's Paddy Doherty was hauled down in the square and he drilled home the penalty as the Sam Maguire Cup went over the border for the first time.

Colm O'Rourke of Meath scored the only goal of the 1987 final against Cork

1976 Dublin 3-8 Kerry 0-10, Croke Park (73,588)

One of the heroes of Dublin's thrilling win against Kerry was Kevin Moran, who later found soccer fame with Manchester United and Ireland. But in the 1976 final Moran tormented the Kerry defence with his pace in a match that was played at 100 miles an hour. John McCarthy opened Dublin's account with a brilliantly worked goal after 15 minutes, and Jimmy Keaveney and Brian Mullins also netted for the Liffeysiders.

1982 Offaly 1-15 Kerry 0-17, Croke Park (62,309)

No side had ever won five All-Ireland football titles in a row but with a couple of minutes to go in the 1982 final it looked as if Kerry were going to make history. The result would have been beyond doubt, had Offaly keeper Martin Furlong not saved a 53rd minute penalty, but it seemed as though they were safe anyway as wing-back Tommy Doyle prepared to collect. However, in stole substitute Seamus Darby to shoot into the back of the Kerry net and shatter their dreams of a fabulous five.

1987 Meath 1-14 Cork 0-11, Croke Park (68,431)

Neither side had enjoyed much success in the years before the 1987 final but it was Meath who lifted the Sam Maguire Cup thanks largely to the experience of veterans Mick Lyons and Colm O'Rourke. What seemed a certain goal for Cork's Jimmy Kerrigan early on was blocked by Lyons, and a few minutes later the only goal of the game was scored by O'Rourke to give the Royals their first All-Ireland triumph since 1967.

1998 Galway 1-14 Kildare 1-10, Croke Park (65,886)

A record television audience of 603,000 watched this All-Ireland Final in which Kildare were trying to win their first title for 70 years. But a Galway side brimming with stars such as Ja Fallon and Michael Donnellan were just too good for Kildare, and their foot passing was a joy to watch. Dermot Earley had given the Lilywhites hope with a first half goal, but Padraig Joyce netted in the second half to give Galway a deserved victory.

2002 Armagh 1-12 Kerry 0-14, Croke Park (79,500)

Armagh's previous two All-Ireland Finals had ended in defeat and they seemed to be heading for a third at half-time against Kerry. They were down four points to Kerry, having missed a first-half penalty and lost John McEntee to concussion. But Oisin McConville's 55th-minute goal turned the game on its head, and Armagh shut out their opponents in the final quarter to secure an emotional win.

The All-Ireland trophy is called the Sam Maguire Cup in honour of the man from West Cork who played for London in the 1900, 1901 and 1903 All-Ireland Finals.

Midfield Maestros

You need to be an all-round action hero to master the midfield.

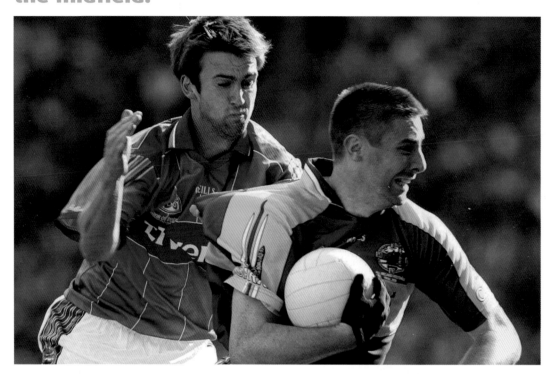

Mayo's Ronan McGarrity and Darragh Ó Sé of Kerry are a couple of midfield maestros

The cliché says a team has to win the midfield battle before they can win the match, and never was a truer word spoken. Take the 2006 season, when Cork beat Kerry in the Munster Final thanks in no small measure to Nicholas Murphy's domination of his Kerry midfield rival Darragh Ó Sé; but in the All-Ireland semi-final it was Ó Sé who controlled the midfield, and Kerry won the day.

Then in the final itself, Ó Sé and his midfield partner Tommy Griffin were just too good for Mayo's Pat Harte and Ronan McGarrity, and Kerry claimed their 34th All-Ireland medal.

So what separates a mediocre midfielder from a majestic one? First, you've got to have all the skills of a defender and an attacker. Solid in the tackle, brave in the block but also capable of producing points. Look at Sean Cavanagh. He has the strength and determination of a top-class defender, but when Tyrone won the 2005 All-Ireland title he scored 12 points from midfield. That's a strike rate that would make any forward proud!

One of the keys to Cavanagh's success is his work rate, and stamina is something all midfielders must have if they want to be a maestro. You have to be constantly on the move, either dropping back to help your defenders stem an attack, or moving forward supporting your attackers as they go for goal.

A good midfielder never stands still – he's always looking for work and always wanting to make sure it's he who controls the centre field.

The Dream Team

NO. 8

Sean Cavanagh

Midfield

TYRONE

Cavanagh made his senior Tyrone debut in 2002 and made an immediate impact as an attacking midfielder, fulfilling the promise he had shown for the Tyrone Minor side that won the 2001 All-Ireland title.

In 2003 Cavanagh was in superb form as Tyrone won their first ever senior All-Ireland title and he was voted Young Player of the Year. When the Red Handers repeated their success in 2005, Cavanagh scored 12 points from midfield.

A high ball specialist, Cavanagh has also played for Ireland in the International Rules against Australia and has won three All-Star awards.

Cavanagh was in great form in 2007, scoring four points when Tyrone beat Monaghan in the Ulster Final.

[False: He's a qualified accountant]

NO. 9

Ciaran Whelan

Midfield

DUBLIN

Veteran 'Whelo' Whelan is rated one of the best high-fielders in the business, yet despite collecting three Leinster Championship titles with the Dubs, the big man has never won an All-Ireland title.

Whelan broke on to the senior scene in 1996, winning his one and only All-Star award in 1999. In recent seasons, however, Whelan has been in sparkling form and he popped up with two points when Dublin beat Laois in the final of the 2007 Leinster Championship.

take a shot!

True or False?
Sean Cavanagh is a qualified architect.

Dublin's Ciaran Whelan

A Safe Pair of Hands

Kicking, tackling, passing, they're all important to be a fantastic football player but the bread and butter of the game is catching. If you can't catch, you're toast!

Arguably the standout moment from the 2006 All-Ireland Final between Kerry and Mayo was Kieran Donaghy's magnificent catch over the head of David Heaney in the ninth minute. Having plucked Tommy Griffin's high ball out of the air, Donaghy turned and sent an unstoppable shot into the back of the Mayo net. Goal!

Catching is so important because that's how you win possession of the ball from the opposition, and so that's how you can build an attack. You're not going to score many goals if you can never keep possession of the ball!

The good news is that catching is one of those skills that can be improved with hard work and practice. And we're going to show you how!

Top training tips

Catching is something you can practise either on your own or with a friend. If you're by yourself, find a wall well away from a window and throw the ball high against it, catching it as it comes down. If your friend is free, start by standing close to one another, say ten metres apart, and the further you move away the better you get!

Move into position

The most important thing to remember as the ball comes your way is to keep your eyes on it, even if an opponent is challenging you. Move into position so that you are underneath the ball, and then as it descends, slightly bend your legs at the knee so you can really spring up and be first to the ball.

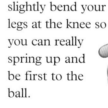

Secure the catch

Push off with your stronger leg and swing your arms up for added lift. Keeping your eyes on the ball (still ignoring everyone around you), extend your arms towards the ball with your hands together so the thumbs are just touching. You should aim to catch the ball just in front of your head and bring it down and into your chest so it is nice and secure.

Kieran Donaghy is recognised as one of the game's great catchers of the high ball

Perfect the Pick-up

Let's say, however, that a high ball is dropped (not by you, obviously, but by someone else!) and bounces loose on the turf. This is where another handling skill is crucial – the pick-up.

GAA rules state that the ball can't be lifted off the ground using the hands and that it must be kicked up into the hands. Relax, it sounds harder than it actually is!

The trick is to flick the ball off the ground with the toe of the boot and in the same motion grasp the ball with both hands. Good players can do this running at full-steam without having to slow down.

Remember to bend your back and knees, and cup your hands in readiness as you run up to the ball. You don't have to flick the ball up high with your foot, just as long as it's your foot that touches the ball before your hands. The moment the ball is in your hands, bring it up to your chest so it's secure and harder for an opponent to dislodge.

Kildare's John Doyle shows how to execute a perfect pick-up

Ulster on the Up

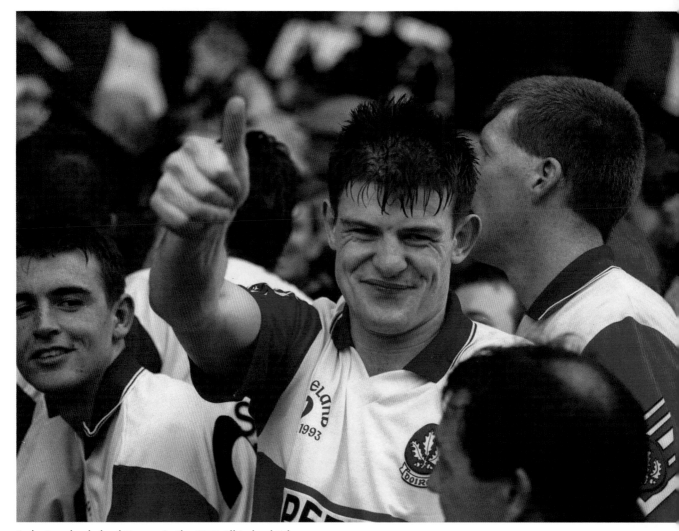

Enda Gormley helped Derry win the 1993 All-Ireland title

It was a long wait, but it was worth it! When Cavan beat Galway in the 1933 All-Ireland Final 45,188 fans braved torrential rain to see the title go to an Ulster side for the first time. Two years later Cavan repeated their success thanks to two goals from Packie Boylan against Kildare, and Ireland knew that Ulster were here to stay!

By the early 1950s, other sides from north of the border were threatening the teams from the south. Antrim lost in the semifinals of the All-Ireland in 1951 and two years later Armagh reached the final but lost to Kerry.

But all the narrow failures were turned to success in the 1960s when Down began to demolish opponents. Inspired by right half-forward Sean O'Neill (No. 10), Down won its first All-Ireland title in 1960 and then went on to lift the Sam Maguire Cup again in 1962 and 1968.

If the 1970s and 1980s were a barren period for Ulster football as Dublin and Kerry dominated, the 1990s was the most glorious decade in their history. Down won the All-Ireland in 1991 and the following year Donegal ran Dublin ragged to win the 1992 All-Ireland title. Then in 1993 Enda Gormley's six points against Cork brought the championship to Derry for the first time, and a year later Down's James MacCartan scored the winning goal in the final against Dublin. Four Ulster victories in four fabulous years!

The new millennium brought fresh triumph for Ulster, with Armagh winning their first Final in 2002 and Tyrone doing likewise the following year in an all-Ulster clash against Armagh.

Tyrone lifted their second title in 2005 thanks to Peter Canavan's first-half goal against Kerry in an emotional game that the Red Hand men dedicated to former captain Cormac McAnallen, who had passed away 18 months earlier. The victory, in what was a pulsating match, was a fitting tribute to the young Tyrone player.

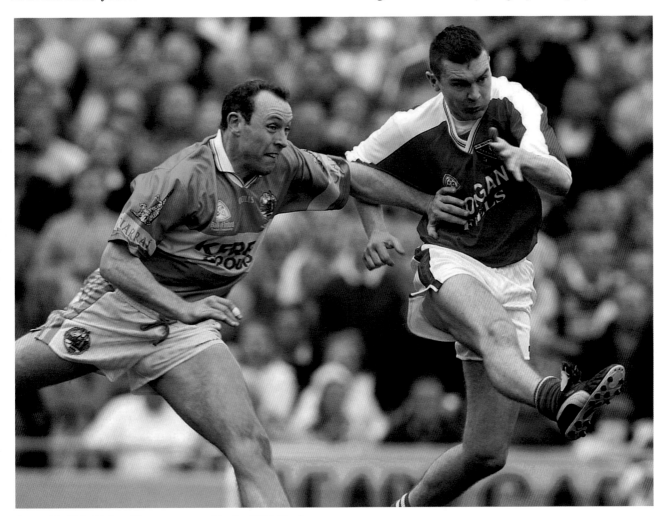

Armagh's Oisin McConville scores a goal in the 2002 Final

The Dream Team

NO. 10

Mark Vaughan

Right half-forward

DUBLIN

Vaughan made his Dubs debut in 2005 against Wexford, having chosen football over soccer (at which he won an Ireland Under-17 cap).

He came on as a substitute in the 2006 All-Ireland semifinal and had a late free well saved by Mayo 'keeper David Clarke that denied Dublin a final spot.

Although a shoulder injury ruled him out of the early part of the 2007 season, Vaughan came storming back, now revelling in his role as a freetaker. In the 2007 Leinster final he netted a fantastic five frees against poor Laois.

[True]

Mark Vaughan

NO. 12

Brian Dooher

Left half-forward

TYRONE

Brian Dooher has one of the highest work rates in football and provides a vital link between defence and attack.

Dooher made his senior Tyrone debut in 1996 at the age of 21 and since then he has gone on to win five Ulster titles, two National Football Leagues and two All-Ireland medals.

He picked up All-Star awards in 2003 and 2005 as well. Not bad for a man who also has a demanding job as a Derry vet!

True or False? Brian Dooher captained Tyrone when they won the 2005 All-Ireland title.

take a shot!

36

Tackle Tips

There are two types of tackle in Gaelic Football and both require timing and tenacity.

The first tackle is the 'shoulder to shoulder' which, as the name suggests, involves leaning your shoulder against your opponent's and trying to unbalance him. Remember you can't use your hip or elbow, and one foot has to stay in contact with the ground throughout. This tackle requires tenacity because your opponent won't want to be tackled so he'll be using his own shoulder to keep you away!

The second tackle is when you try to knock the ball out of your opponent's hand with the open palm of your hand. There are three important rules to remember when trying to dislodge the ball this way:

1. **You can't use your fist**
2. **You can only use one hand**
3. **You can't pull the ball from your opponent's grasp**

This tackle requires timing because if you go for the ball, miss, and strike your opponent, then the referee will probably award a free kick against you. So watch the ball and when you do decide to try to dislodge it, do it quickly otherwise your opponent will shield the ball with his body.

Longford's Kevin Smith tackles Damien Healy of Westmeath

You can also try to block an opponent's kick as he strikes the ball with his feet. Make sure you don't come into contact with the kicker, but rather try to get your hands in the way of the ball as he kicks it. If you're successful and the ball bounces loose, then the ball is back in open play.

did you know?

In women's football the 'shoulder to shoulder' tackle is forbidden, so you can only dispossess your opponent by knocking the ball out of her hands.

Gaelic Girls

Women's football is one of the fastest growing sports in Ireland these days and the rivalry is as red-hot as it is in the men's game.

Amazingly, women's football only began to be played seriously in 1974 when representatives from Galway, Kerry, Offaly and Tipperary met at a hotel in Thurles and agreed to set up official competitions. It didn't take long to catch on, and the 2006 All-Ireland Championship was watched by 25,000 fans; another 175,000 tuned in to see it live on TV.

In the early days Kerry reigned supreme and thanks to star players such as Mary Jo Curran and Annette Walsh, they won nine consecutive All-Ireland Championships between 1982 and 1990.

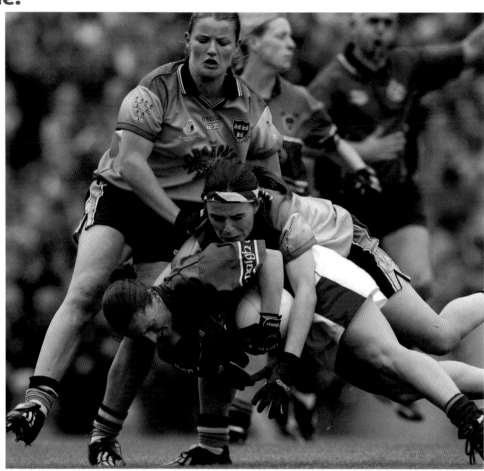

Diane O'Hora of Mayo comes under pressure from Dublin in the 2003 Final

Women's football is very similar to men's, although matches last only 60 minutes, not 70. Also, goal kicks are kicked from the hand and players are allowed to pick up the ball directly from the ground.

But when it comes to drama and rivalry, the women's game is as exciting as the men's. Waterford and Monaghan were the two top teams in the 1990s, but then along came Mayo. They won four All-Ireland Championships between 1999 and 2003, with only Laois's triumph in 2001 preventing Mayo from making it five out of five.

If players such as goalkeeping great Denise Horan, fantastic forward Cora Staunton and the Heffernan sisters (Christina and Marcella) helped Mayo become magic, then something similar has happened to Cork during the last few years.

The Rebelettes of Cork had never even reached an All-Ireland Final before 2005, but that year the ladies of Cork beat Galway to become champs. The following year in 2006 they retained the title with a victory over Armagh.

Cork have strength everywhere, from Angela Walsh in defence to Juliette Murphy in midfield, not forgetting the frightening firepower up front of Nollaig Cleary and Mary O'Connor.

The 16 teams who competed in the 2007 All-Ireland Championship provided some great entertainment before Cork and Mayo contested a thrilling finale in Croke Park in September. No wonder that women's football now has over 110,000 members in over 1000 clubs around the world.

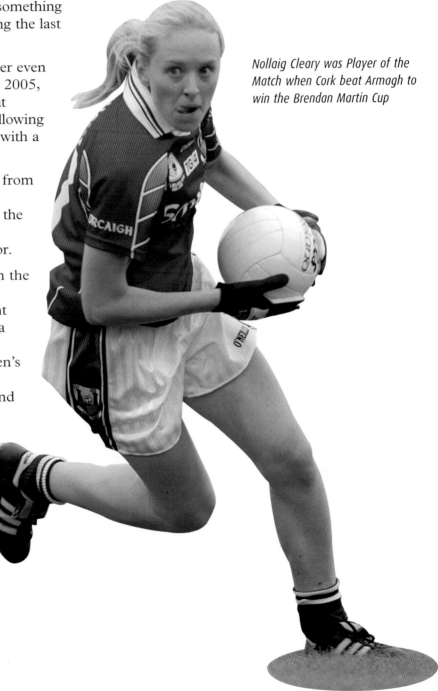

Nollaig Cleary was Player of the Match when Cork beat Armagh to win the Brendan Martin Cup

The women's All-Ireland Championship trophy is named after Brendan Martin, who was one of the driving forces behind establishing the women's championship in the early 1970s.

The Gaelic Greats

Which is the greatest Gaelic Football team ever? It's impossible to know because every fan has their favourite, but in 1999 a panel of GAA experts selected their Team of the Millennium. Were they right? Read on and see if you agree!

Goalkeeper: Dan O'Keefe, Kerry

Born in Fermoy, County Cork, in 1907, 'Danno' appeared in ten All-Ireland Finals in the 1930s and 1940s with Kerry and was on the winning side seven times.

Right corner-back: Enda Colleran, Galway

Colleran was at the heart of the Galway defence when they won three consecutive All-Ireland Championship titles in the 1960s, and he later managed the Galway side.

Full-back: Joe Keohane, Kerry

Joe Keohane won his first senior provincial medal in 1936 and he finished his great career with five All-Ireland medals. Few full-backs could ever boast a better long kick.

Left corner-back: Sean Flanagan, Mayo

A politician and footballer, Flanagan captained Mayo when they won the All-Ireland Championship in 1950 and 1951 and he also won two National Football League titles.

Right half-back: Sean Murphy, Kerry

A doctor and a versatile footballer who won the first of his All-Ireland titles as a midfielder in 1953. Later Murphy won two more as a right half-back and was named Footballer of the Year in 1959.

Centre-back: John Joe (J J) O'Reilly, Cavan

A genius of a centre back, O'Reilly was also an inspirational captain and led Cavan to All-Ireland glory in 1947 and a year later when they beat Mayo in the 1948 Final.

Martin O'Connell won three All-Ireland titles with Meath

Left half-back: Martin O'Connell, Meath

O'Connell was an attacking wing back who played a large part in helping Meath win All-Ireland titles in 1987, 1988 and 1996. He also won six Leinster medals.

Midfield: Mick O'Connell, Kerry

O'Connell had all the skills in a glittering career and won eight Munster titles in a row (12 in all). The first of his All-Ireland titles came in 1959, and the fourth and last in 1970 against Meath.

Midfield: Tommy Murphy, Laois

Nicknamed the 'Boy Wonder', Murphy made his senior debut for Laois in 1937 aged 16 and became a great midfielder. He won Leinster provincial medals in 1937, 1938 and 1946.

Right half-forward: Pat Spillane, Kerry

Pat Spillane won eight All-Ireland titles with Kerry between 1975 and 1986, and also collected nine All-Star awards, a record that was fitting reward for his work rate and fitness.

Centre-forward: Sean Purcell, Galway

'The Master' is considered the greatest of all centre-forwards for his athleticism and balance. He won an All-Ireland title with Galway in 1956 and helped the side claim seven Connacht titles between 1954 and 1963.

Left half-forward: Sean O'Neill, Down

Sean O'Neill was a goal-scoring great for Down during their glory days of the 1960s when they won three All-Ireland titles and three National League medals.

Right corner-forward: Mikey Sheehy, Kerry

Sheehy won eight All-Ireland titles with Kerry between 1975 and 1986, and his ability to score goals from frees and play was unique. His brilliance was rewarded with seven All-Star awards.

Full-forward: Tommy Langan, Mayo

Langan was a tall, lean, scoring machine for Mayo in the late '40s and early '50s. His goals contributed to them winning Connacht titles and two All-Ireland crowns.

Left half-forward: Kevin Heffernan, Dublin

The great Dublin team of the

Mikey Sheehy was a seven All-Stars sensation with Kerry

1950s was based on the St Vincent's side and no one played a bigger part than Heffernan. Blessed with searing pace and a superb sidestep, Heffernan captained Dublin to All-Ireland glory in 1958 and enjoyed great success with the Dubs in the 1970s, as their manager.

The Dream Team

NO.

11

Alan Brogan

Centre half-forward

DUBLIN

Growing up the son of a football legend can't have been easy for Dubs' Alan Brogan but the lightning-quick centre half-forward has established his own reputation as a points machine.

Dad Bernard, a prolific scorer for Dublin in the 1970s, must be proud of his son's exploits, especially the nine points he scored for Ireland in the International Rules Football win against Australia in 2004.

In the 2005 All-Ireland Championship Brogan scored two goals and 20 points and the following year his consistent good form was rewarded with his first All-Star award. Brogan was in cracking form in 2007, netting one of Dublin's three goals in the 3-14 1-14 defeat of Laois in the Leinster final.

[True]

take a shot!

True or False?
Alan has a younger brother, Bernard, who is also in the Dublin squad.

Fearsome Forwards

An eye for the goal and pace to burn – that's what makes a forward fearsome.

Remember, the ball-carrier can score a point by striking the ball over the crossbar using his hand, but he's not allowed to strike the ball into the goal unless the ball is in flight.

Galway's Declan Meehan, scorer of a wonder goal in 2000

Think back over the last few All-Ireland finals and what tends to stick in the memory? Brilliant blocks, super saves or great goals? It's the glorious goals: moments like Kieran Donaghy's goal for Kerry against Mayo in 2006 or Declan Meehan's net-buster for Galway against Kerry in 2000.

But there are a number of factors that make a forward feared by the opposition defence. Yes, an eye for goal is important – and that means not just getting into a good shooting position but then delivering a shot that is on target.

Of course, you can practise your shooting skills whenever you like, but positional play is harder. First, you need to be fit and fast, so you can pull defenders out of position and create a goalscoring opportunity by moving your marker around. And that opportunity could be for you, or a team-mate.

Good teamwork is essential for any forward. You should know where your team-mates are and be prepared to pass to them if you think they have a better chance of scoring.

Lastly, the most frightening forwards are those who are just as deadly with their feet as they are with their hands. That makes life more difficult for defenders. So if you feel you're stronger scoring goals with your hand than your foot, get practising and cause double trouble for the opposition defence.

The Dream Team

NO. 13
Colm Cooper
Right full-forward

KERRY

'Gooch', as the 24-year-old Cooper is better known, has been terrorising opposition defences since 2002, although not even his attacking skills could prevent Armagh beating Kerry in that year's All-Ireland Final.

In 2004, however, Cooper got his hands on all All-Ireland medal as he inspired Kerry to an awesome win against Mayo with a terrific goal.

The next year the Kingdom were again in the final but Cooper was injured early on and could do nothing as his side slumped to defeat against Tyrone. In 2007 he was in great form, scoring 1-5 as Kerry beat Cork in the All-Ireland Final.

[False: He's the youngest]

NO. 15
Conor Mortimer
Left full-forward

MAYO

The charismatic Conor Mortimer was last season's top scorer in the Championship with 1-32, but despite his goal-scoring stunts he couldn't prevent Mayo losing to Kerry in the All-Ireland Final.

It was Mortimer's second final defeat, mirroring Mayo's 2004 loss to Kerry. Nonetheless, his consistent performances in 2006 were rewarded with his first All-Star award, further proof that the extrovert Mortimer has matured since the late 1990s when he was controversially omitted from the Mayo side for the 1999 All-Ireland minor final for disciplinary reasons.

take a shot!

True or False?
Conor, left, is the eldest
of the three footballing
Mortimer brothers.

The Great Stadiums

Stadiums are to sport what theatres are to plays, and Gaelic Football is fortunate to have some truly awe-inspiring stadiums that create a special atmosphere of their own.

Croke Park in Dublin is one of the world's great stadiums

The most famous of them all is Croke Park, or 'Croker' to give the famous old stadium its affectionate nickname. Originally called 'Jones's Road', the venue first hosted an All-Ireland football final in 1895, but it wasn't until 1913 that the GAA bought the 14 acres for £3,645 (equivalent to about €500,000 today).

The GAA renamed the ground Croke Park in honour of Archbishop Thomas Croke, the first patron of the GAA. In 1913 'Croker' consisted of two stands and grassy banks, but over the years the GAA developed it into a magnificent stadium. The Hogan stand was opened in 1924, the Cusack stand in 1938 and the Nally stand was built in 1952.

In the 1980s the GAA decided Croke Park needed to be updated and work began to redevelop the stadium. It was finally finished in 2005 when the new Hill 16 terrace was opened. The capacity of Croke Park is now an incredible 82,500 and its floodlights mean matches can be played in the evening.

Croke Park is the fourth biggest sports stadium in Europe after the Nou Camp (Barcelona), Wembley (London) and the San Siro (Milan).

The Fitzgerald Stadium in Killarney with Kerry mountains in the background

There are plenty of other impressive GAA stadiums in Ireland apart from 'Croker'. Semple Stadium, in Thurles, County Tipperary, is the second largest stadium in Ireland with a capacity of 53,500 and is second only to Croke Park in great GAA stadiums. It was built in 1910 and named after Thurles' brilliant hurling champion Tom Semple.

Páirc Uí Chaoimh Stadium in Cork, which opened in 1976, has a capacity of 43,500 but the Cork County GAA board hope soon to increase that figure by 5,000 by redeveloping part of the ground.

The Gaelic Grounds in Limerick City was built on old farmground in the 1920s but like many other GAA grounds it was updated as crowd numbers increased. The stadium now holds 50,000 spectators but still retains its famous red-hot atmosphere.

Pearse Stadium in Galway was constructed in the 1950s on an area known by locals as The Boggers because it was so wet and boggy. Like Croke Park, Pearse Stadium has been given a recent facelift and it reopened in 2003 with a capacity of 34,000.

McHale Park stadium in Castlebar, County Mayo, gets its name from John McHale, archbishop of Tuam for many years in the 19th century. It was built in the 1930s but is now undergoing extensive redevelopment which will raise its capacity to over 40,000.

The Dream Team

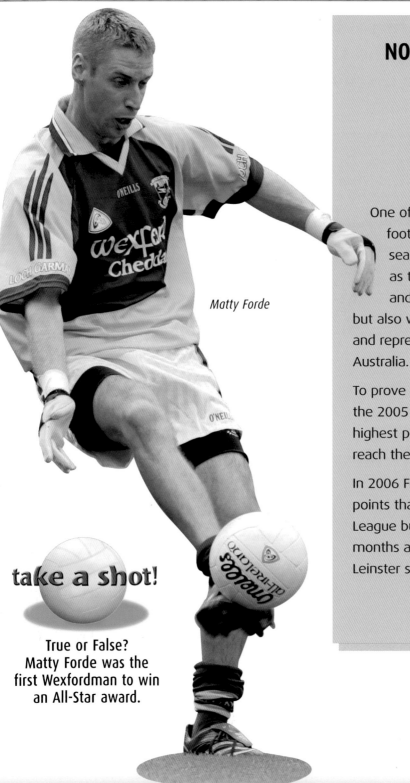

Matty Forde

take a shot!

True or False?
Matty Forde was the
first Wexfordman to win
an All-Star award.

NO. **14**

Matty Forde

Full-forward

WEXFORD

One of the hottest forwards in football, Forde had an unforgettable season in 2004, not only finishing as top-scorer in the National league and the All-Ireland Championship, but also winning his first All-Star award and representing Ireland against Australia.

To prove it wasn't a fluke, Forde ended the 2005 season as the National League's highest points scorer, helping Wexford reach the final.

In 2006 Forde again racked up more points than anyone else in the National League but was later banned for three months after a stamping incident in the Leinster semifinal defeat to Offaly.

[true]

The Record Breakers

Broken legs, broken arms – football can be a dangerous game at times but the one thing no player minds breaking is a record. Read on to discover some of football's remarkable records.

The oldest player to appear in an All Ireland Final was Kildare's Larry Hussey Cribben. He was 41 when he helped the Lilywhites beat Galway in 1919.

The record attendance for an All-Ireland football match was the 90,556 who piled into Croke Park in 1961 to see Down beat Offaly.

Two players share the scoring record in an All-Ireland Final of 2–6. They are Dublin's Jimmy Keaveney in 1977 and Kerry's Mikey Sheehy in 1979.

One unwanted record came in the 1983 All-Ireland Final between Dublin and Galway when a record four players were sent off – three Dubliners and one Tribesman. Amazingly, Dublin still managed to win the match!

Similarly, the first player to be sent off in an All-Ireland Final was a Dubliner in the 1908 match against London. Fortunately for the offender, newspaper reports didn't name him for fear of causing

A record TV audience of 887,000 watched Tyrone win the 2005 Final

embarrassment and so his name isn't in the Hall of Shame. Even better, the Dubs won the game!

The most one-sided All-Ireland Final (after 1895 when a goal was reduced to three points) was when Tipperary 2-17 thrashed Galway 0-1 at Terenure in 1900. That's a whopping 22 points!

Kerry have won the most All-Ireland titles with 35. Their first victory came in 1903 and their most recent was the 3-13 1-9 thrashing of Cork in 2007.

Kerry are one of two sides to have won four consecutive All-Ireland titles. Kingdom have done it twice, in fact, between 1929 and 1932 and then again between 1978 and

1981. Wexford managed four on the trot between 1915 and 1918.

Tyrone's victory against Kerry in the 2005 All-Ireland Final attracted a record television audience of 887,000.

Declan O'Sullivan and Colm Cooper lift the Sam Maguire Cup in 2006 as Kerry celebrate another All-Ireland title